MAY I
WASH
YOUR
FEET?

MAY I WASH YOUR FEET?

Joy Haney

May I Wash Your Feet?

by Joy Haney

©1991 Word Aflame Press
Hazelwood, MO 63042

Cover Design by Tim Agnew

All Scripture quotations in this book are from the King James Version of the Bible unless otherwise identified.

Printed in United States of America

Printed by

Library of Congress Cataloging-in-Publication Data

Haney, Joy, 1942–
May I wash your feet?/Joy Haney.
p. cm.
Includes bibliographical references.
ISBN 0-932581-87-0
1. Service (Theology) 2. Christian life—1960–
I. Title.
BT738.4.H364 1991
248.4—dc20

91-21855
CIP

Contents

Acknowledgment

In 1984, I was impressed to write a book on servant-hood. That same year I shared this thought with the wife of a guest evangelist ministering at Christian Life Center. In response, Thelma Hightower told me that during the altar service that night after she had praised the Lord, she saw a vision of the Lord sitting on a throne. He was surrounded by a glorious, shining light, and a woman was kneeling at his feet asking, "May I wash Your feet?"

I said excitedly, "That's the perfect title for the book!" She very unselfishly let me use this title, for which I am grateful to her.

Introduction

As the lovely young lady on the other end of the telephone spoke with heavy concern for a certain friend, I realized that this was no ordinary phone call. As much as possible I shut out the noise of the stereo, the children, and their friends, and I tuned into what she was saying.

She talked at length, baring her heart to me as her voice broke, and my eyes filled with tears. She related how in the past several months she had been broken, cried much, and felt so alone. Her husband, being sensitive to her need, had moved her office back home so that, after sending the children off to school, she could have her morning prayer before beginning her work.

She said at first she felt angry at God and others because of her loneliness. "Why am I alone in such a large crowd?" she cried. God spoke to her to reach out to others, for they were feeling just like her. She asked God to make her sensitive to the needs of others, and He began to lay people on her heart. She would pray for them and call them, and they would tell her how much they needed a friend.

After hanging up the phone, I mused on what had happened. She had spoken of how blessed her world had become. What had changed her world? It was simply an attitude change. Instead of saying, "Serve me!" she started saying, "Let me serve you." She developed a servant's spirit.

This incident occurred in 1987. I had started this book in 1984 but set it aside for other writing assignments that seemed to signal for my attention. Every once in a while, I would get it out and work on it, but I never felt the assurance of the right time to finish it. I felt strongly that the year 1990 was the time to finish the book.

Here is my gift to you after learning from some bitter experiences that the life of the servant is the most blessed, happiest, and rewarding.

Let us consider some of the characteristics of servanthood, and how important it is, for it is impossible to live for God without being a servant!

CHAPTER 1

The Great Servant Speaks

Harsh, blackened shadows became the backdrop for the solitary figure as he furtively made his way to the closed meeting. Unrest permeated the air, making the young man tense and his senses alert. Upon hearing measured footsteps behind him, he paused and flattened himself against the stone wall of the outer court by one of the city's prominent dwelling places.

As he waited for the footsteps to pass by, the air was suddenly punctuated by the anguished cry of a commoner being assaulted by a soldier. Breathing heavily as fear fastened itself upon him, the young man listened for the footsteps to continue on by him, when he realized the footsteps had stopped.

Questions raced through his brain, which was paralyzed with fear. What happened to the footsteps? Was someone waiting to ambush him? As the city became somewhat quieter he knew he had to make a decision. He would miss the important meeting he was supposed to attend if he did not venture forth, but on the other hand he did not want to risk being robbed or killed. He decided to make a wild dash and start running since he was only three blocks away from his destination. Very swiftly and quietly he ran as if a pack of dogs were after him. After two blocks of heavy running he looked back, and upon hearing and seeing no one, he slowed down and walked quickly the rest of the way.

As he arrived at his destination and started up the stairs to the upper room that had been supplied by one of the good men of the city, he thought with excitement about tonight's meeting. It was to be the Passover dinner with Jesus and His disciples. He opened the door and went in, finding everyone else already there. As the disciples greeted him he quickly found his place at the long table.

It was not long until conversation flowed. Great things were being discussed when suddenly strife came among them. They began to try to decide who would be the greatest among them (Luke 22:24).

Jesus turned to them in the damp room that was uncluttered by much furniture and uttered these words that still ring and reverberate down through the corridors of time:

He that is greatest among you, let him be as the younger; and he that is chief, as he that doth serve (Luke 22:26).

In doing so, He reiterated what He had taught them earlier:

Whosoever will be great among you, let him be your minister; and whosoever will be chief among you, let him be your servant (Matthew 20:26-27).

But he that is greatest among you shall be your servant (Matthew 23:11).

And whosoever of you will be the chiefest, shall be servant of all (Mark 10:44).

Jesus not only spoke of being a servant, He showed them what it meant. He rose from the table, took a towel, and girded himself with it. After that He poured water into a basin, began to wash the disciples' feet, and then wiped them with the towel. (See John 13:1-17).

As they sat there with stunned expressions, some with dismay, Jesus came to Peter. Peter asked Him if He was going to wash his feet also. Jesus told him that he would not understand what was happening right then but that in time he would understand.

This answer did not satisfy Peter. He emphatically told Jesus that he would never allow Him to wash his feet. Jesus answered Peter, "If I wash thee not, thou hast no part with me" (John 13:8).

Peter, as quickly as he had denied, promptly affirmed to Christ that he did want a part of Him. He said, "Lord, not my feet only, but also my hands and my head" (John 13:9).

After Jesus finished washing the disciples' feet, He sat down and asked them a question: "Know ye what I have done to you?" (John 13:12).

No one answered; they just looked at Him. This was something new. They had been with Him for three years, and He had never done anything like this before. This was strange. As they remained quiet, He went on to tell them why He had done it:

Ye call me Master and Lord: and ye say well; for so I am. If I then, your Lord and Master, have washed your feet, ye also ought to wash one another's feet. For I have given you an example, that ye should do as I have done to you. Verily, verily, I say unto you, The servant is not greater than his lord; neither he that is sent greater than he that sent him. If ye know these things, happy are ye if ye do them (John 13:13-17).

There were those words again—about the servant. Some of them wondered how they could be happy being a servant. He had been telling them some different things lately. He had talked about going away; now He was talking about washing feet and becoming a servant. One among them could not accept this message. He wanted out. He exited out the door soon after and never again had the same relationship with Christ. What happened to him? He spent the end of his days hanging on a rope. His decision not to conform to the Master's words certainly did not bring him satisfaction.

There are still those who choose the route that Judas chose. Recently, while I was preparing for our church's ladies retreat in the mountains, one of the sisters told me that God had been speaking to her about footwashing. When she told me her experience, I felt a quickening in my spirit and felt that God wanted us to partake of foot-washing at our retreat. This was her feeling also.

We did not tell anyone, as we did not want to keep anyone from coming. Once we were there, word got out that on Saturday morning we were to have footwashing, and there were a few vacant chairs.

When I stood and read the thirteenth chapter of John preceding this service, a special visitation from God settled over the congregation of ladies. Groups of five or six formed a circle, and each person washed the lady's feet next to her. After washing and drying the feet and praying for one another, we embraced.

It is impossible to describe what happened. Tears flowed like rivers. Women who had not spoken to one another for quite some time embraced each other. We felt as if we were walking through swirls of love. The love was so thick it seemed like an ocean of care, forgiveness, and divine love. Some ladies told me that they had been afraid and almost had not come to the service, but with tears running down their cheeks, they said they would not have missed it for anything. It was one of the greatest services they had ever been in. They said they felt so clean.

It had been several years since I had participated in a footwashing service, but the sight of those ladies washing one another's feet spoke volumes to me. As I knelt and washed the feet of Nona Freeman, missionary to Africa for forty years, the impression came to me very strongly that this was the true attitude of a servant.

It was as if I heard His voice again: "But he that is greatest among you shall be your servant. And whosoever shall exalt himself shall be abased; and he that shall humble himself shall be exalted'' (Matthew 23:11-12).

How does this message apply to us in everyday life? To address this question let me share something that happened to me in 1987.

CHAPTER 2

The Actions of a Servant

It was early morning, and I was downstairs in my husband's office on July 11, 1987. Since it was summertime we had opened the windows the night before so the upstairs would cool off. One of the wonderful things about California is that even if it is hot in the day, it always cools off at night. The birds woke me up this morning, but I did not awake with a happy feeling. Something had happened the night before that made me feel very bad.

The Lord started dealing with me just moments after it had happened. I was standing in line at the grocery store, and there were long lines of people everywhere. As I neared my turn at the checkout stand, I noticed an elderly woman edging her cart in from the side. Those of us in line were moving toward the register, and she was crowding in from the side. Everyone clearly understood that she was not in line. She got to where I was and almost touched me with her basket as she tried to break in line. She was not belligerent, just an older woman trying to get in a long line. She may not have been right, but I certainly was not right in what I did, because the Lord dealt with me over my actions.

I simply stayed close to the man and lady in front of me and did not let the woman in. I started putting groceries on the counter before she could make her way in. It was the natural thing to do, but it was the wrong thing to do. It was not the attitude of a servant of Jesus Christ. I felt so bad when I looked back and saw that the people behind me had let her in.

When I got to the car I prayed, "O God, forgive me. I failed you. I want your Spirit to flow through me, and yet I still have obstructions in the way."

That very morning the Lord had met with me in such a wonderful way, and there I was acting carnally only sixteen hours later. I told my husband, who had waited in the car, about the situation. We discussed the way I felt, but I still felt bad. Upon arriving home we put the groceries away, and I fixed everyone a late snack. Because of weariness from a day that had been filled with so many plans for our daughter's soon-coming wedding, I fell asleep almost as soon as my head touched the pillow.

About 5:00 A.M. the next morning, one particular bird persisted in waking me up, and immediately the memory of the previous night's happening came to my mind. The Lord was still dealing with me. He brought to my mind the incident in the Scriptures when He said, "Inasmuch as ye have done it unto one of the least of these my brethren, ye have done it unto me" (Matthew 25:40). Then the title of this chapter flashed through my mind: the actions of a servant. I tried to reason back and say that verse meant doing things for other Christians, but He brought to my mind verse 36: "I was in prison, and ye came unto me." I thought, Now who are those in the prisons? Not many Christians.

I had started this book and then filed it away, but that morning I felt so forcefully the Lord telling me that it was time to work on it some more. But it was Saturday morning, so instead I closed the windows and drapes to try to shut out the loud bird call. I then lay back down, pulled the covers around me as the morning chill pervaded the room, and tried to go back to sleep.

It was no use; the call of the Lord won out. I picked up my paper, Bible, and pen, put my robe on, went down to the office, and opened the Bible to Matthew 25:31-46, while big tears coursed down my cheeks.

Whispering to Him I said, "Lord, I pray for You to use me and to help me dream of great things, whenever You want to work through me in the everyday happenings of life."

Then I remembered Paul's words: "For I know that in me (that is, in my flesh,) dwelleth no good thing: for to will is present with me; but how to perform that which is good I find not. For the good that I would I do not: but the evil which I would not, that I do" (Romans 7:18-19). "There is none righteous, no, not one" (Romans 3:10). "That the righteousness of the law might be fulfilled in us, who walk not after the flesh, but after the Spirit" (Romans 8:4). "But now being made free from sin, and become servants to God, ye have your fruit unto holiness, and the end everlasting life" (Romans 6:22).

There was the answer; it screamed out at me: we must "become servants to God." That was the secret— submitting the flesh, the will, the human spirit to the only righteous One and letting Him work His righteousness in our lives. If believers are to bring a hurting, crying world to God and salvation, it is essential that Christians everywhere adopt the servant spirit, saying, "Let me wash your feet."

The actions of a servant are not haughty, pushy, or self-seeking, but they are motivated by humility, submissiveness, and giving preference to others. Even though we have a treasure within our earthen vessel and are God's chosen people, we are never to glory in ourselves or become puffed up and demand our own way. Rather, we must remain a humble vessel so that His glory will be able to shine through us. It is not the vessel the world wants to see; it is what is inside the vessel.

Our actions are the only Bible some people read. We should ask ourselves, "What did the neighbor, clerk, motorist, stranger, and wrongdoer see in me today? Did they see Christ, or did they see temper or carnality?" Like John the Baptist, we must confess, "He must increase, but I must decrease" (John 3:30). Oh, that the world would see Christ in us!

Jesus said forcefully, "Let your light so shine before men, that they may see your good works, and glorify your Father which is in heaven" (Matthew 5:16). In order for Him to be glorified we must follow His teachings, which are foreign to the natural man:

Ye have heard that it hath been said, Thou shalt love thy neighbour, and hate thine enemy. But I say unto you, Love your enemies, bless them that curse you, do good to them that hate you, and pray for them which despitefully use you, and persecute you; that ye may be the children of your Father which is in heaven: for he maketh his sun to rise on the evil and on the good, and sendeth rain on the just and on the unjust. For if ye love them which love you, what reward have ye? do not even the publicans the same? And if ye salute your brethren only, what do ye more than others? do not even the publicans so? Be ye therefore perfect, even as your Father which is in heaven is perfect (Matthew 5:43-48).

It is easy to love and serve those who are doing the things we think they should do, or who are smiling and being good to us; but the test of true Christianity is being kind to the evil. H. W. Beecher said, "There's not much practical Christianity in the man who lives on better terms with angels and seraphs than with his children, servants and neighbors."[2]

Stephen Merritt, the great mission worker who was himself delivered from the depths of a sinful life, once gave a supper in his mission to which all outcast and homeless men were invited. After attending the gathering, he took up his hat to go and found that some of the men, in a prankster spirit, had half filled his hat with bacon rinds, pieces of crust, and bones. He was furious for a moment, and in a towering rage he mounted a chair and delivered a speech. He stormed at the tramps, threatened to call the police, and berated them for their ingratitude.

Then suddenly there flashed into his mind the words of the Scripture: Love "suffereth long, and is kind . . . is not easily provoked . . . beareth all things" (I Corinthians 13:4-7). The Holy Spirit rebuked him, the fit of temper passed, and contrition filled his heart. He then and there apologized in all humility, telling them he knew he had grieved his Lord. He then invited them all to another dinner the following night. The jokers at once acknowledged their prank, and the next night forty men repented.

The fragrance of Christ must fill our being and overpower the stench of evil. G. Campbell Morgan related that he often went into the home of a man who entertained him, and in one room he always detected a strong fragrance of roses. He said to his host one day, "I wish you would tell me why, whenever I come into this room, I smell the fragrance of roses."

The gentlemen smiled and replied, "Ten years ago I was in the Holy Land, and while there I bought a small tube of attar of roses. It was wrapped in cotton wool, and as I was standing here unpacking it, suddenly I broke the bottle. I put the broken container, cotton wool and all, into the vase on the mantel."

He then walked to the beautiful vase and lifted the lid, and the fragrance of roses filled the room. The fragrance had permeated the clay of the vase, and it was impossible for someone to enter the room without being conscious of it.

The goal of every Christian should be for the Rose of Sharon to so fill the clay vessel of the human house that His fragrance would linger on and on and ever influence the surroundings.

As Jesus became a servant and allowed His body to be broken so that His Spirit could fill our house, let us become a servant to Him, our Master, and to His cause. Let our daily attitude be "May I wash Your feet," not only in word but also in action.

CHAPTER 3

Servants in the Dark

In one of the famous lace shops of Brussels there used to be certain rooms devoted to the spinning of the finest and most delicate lace patterns. The rooms were completely darkened, except for the light from one very small window falling directly upon the pattern. There was only one spinner in the room, and he sat where the narrow stream of light would fall upon the threads he was weaving. The guide who took visitors through the place would tell them, "We secure our choicest products by this method. Lace is always more delicately and beautifully woven when the worker himself is in the dark and only his pattern is in the light."[1] The most valuable lace was made when the worker stayed in the dark.

So it is in our spiritual life. John the Baptist had keen insight into this spiritual truth when he cried, "He must increase, but I must decrease" (John 3:30). Jesus uttered this truth to the Greeks who came to worship at the feast. He said of Himself, "And I, if I be lifted up from the earth, will draw all men unto me" (John 12:32). The light must shine on Him, the pattern.

How do we stay in the dark? The world will see us physically, but they can see something in us to let them know that Christ lives within. Our own selfish desires will decrease as He increases in our lives. Self will submit to a higher motive or calling even when it is not convenient to do so.

Dr. Cortland Myers boarded a train en route to a city where he was to speak. Hoping to prepare his messages while on the train, he spread out his books over two seats and began to study. A large lady and four dirty children were seated behind him. One boy started climbing on the back of Dr. Myers's seat and putting dirty fingers on his collar. He was minded to put the boy in his place, but instead Dr. Myers bought some candy for all the children.

Hours went by and he was unable to work on his sermons; instead he spent his time telling stories to the urchins. A man who was about to leave the train came to Dr. Myers, and with tears in his eyes, thanked him for his kindness to these children. He said the people in the car had been watching and saying, "That's real Christianity."

"I do not understand," said Dr. Myers. He was told that the old lady was the grandmother. The mother was in a coffin in the baggage car.

"Be careful how you travel," was Dr. Myers's advice. "Remember that others are watching to see if your Christianity is all talk!"[3]

"Humility like darkness reveals the heavenly lights," wrote Henry David Thoreau.[2]

One evening in the golden sunset a young boy walked with confusion in his heart to a mobile home in a little trailer park. He knocked at the door in an urgent way, and a little gray-haired woman opened the door. She had a smile on her face and a twinkle in her eyes as she said, "Come in."

It was not long after being inside that he poured out his troubles. After listening intently, she, in her customary way, said, "Let's pray." What a difference her prayer made! The air cleared, and his troubles did not seem as bad as they were.

She had learned to shine the light on Jesus while she ministered to the one in need. Those who knew her made a steady stream to her door for counsel, for encouragement, or just to talk. She included Jesus in all of her conversations. When people thought of her, they thought more about the pattern than about the worker. She influenced many lives. God's kingdom increased because of her ability to decrease as she magnified Christ.

The lace workers in Brussels worked in solitude, but we work among people daily. How can we focus attention on Jesus instead of our problems and shortcomings? A good example is found in the story of Nehemiah.

When Hanani visited Nehemiah and told him of the affliction and reproach of the Jews and that the walls of Jerusalem were torn down, Nehemiah wept. A burden was born in his heart, and he mourned, fasted, and prayed before the God of heaven.

Soon afterward Nehemiah, the king's cupbearer, took wine to King Artaxerxes. The king noticed that Nehemiah was sad and asked him about it. As Nehemiah unfolded the story to the king and queen, God gave him favor. The king gave him leave of absence to rebuild the walls and also supplied the material to do the job.

This was a great undertaking for one man, but Nehemiah put emphasis upon his God and not upon himself. After he gathered the men he needed for the job, they left in the night to view their future project. Here are his words: "I told them of the hand of my God which was good upon me; as also the king's words that he had spoken unto me. And they said, Let us rise up and build. So they strengthened their hands for this good work. But when Sanballat the Horonite, and Tobiah the servant, the Ammonite, and Geshem the Arabian, heard it, they laughed us to scorn, and despised us, and said, What is this thing that ye do? will ye rebel against the king? Then answered I them, and said unto them, The God of heaven, he will prosper us; therefore we his servants will arise and build" (Nehemiah 2:18-20).

Later when Sanballat and Tobiah fought against them, Nehemiah again put emphasis on his God. "And I looked, and rose up, and said unto the nobles, and to the rulers, and to the rest of the people, Be not ye afraid of them: remember the Lord, which is great and terrible, and fight for your brethren, your sons, and your daughters, your wives, and your houses. And it came to pass, when our enemies heard that it was known unto us, and God had brought their counsel to nought, that we returned all of us to the wall, every one unto his work" (Nehemiah 4:14-15).

All through the long ordeal of mocking, craftiness, and heartlessness on the part of the enemy, not once did Nehemiah rise up in his own flesh, but he leaned heavily upon his God. Finally when the wall was finished the enemies had to acknowledge what God had done: "And it came to pass, that when all our enemies heard thereof, and all the heathen that were about us saw these things, they were much cast down in their own eyes: for they perceived that this work was wrought of our God" (Nehemiah 6:16).

Enough flesh is displayed in Hollywood and the media to paper a wall around the world. But a fleshly display does not point desperate, hurt, and lonely people to the light; it only intimidates and depresses them. People want to attain something valuable in a world of plastic, instant products, and throwaways, and the only thing of true, everlasting value is Jesus. May the church hide behind the Cross and let God's light shine through human vessels so that they will glorify Christ.

"There was once a poor Irish peasant who could scarcely read, yet he loved to gather his neighbors together in his old barn and try to read the Bible to them and preach the gospel. In the little company was a young stranger. He was many miles from his cultured home where he had often heard the story of Christ's saving love, but he had never been willing to yield his heart.

"However, there was something in the presentation of the truth by this stammering backwoods preacher that carried deep conviction to his heart. . . . It was none other than Augustus Toplady who went forth from the unique sanctuary to become the mighty teacher of the Scriptures and the author of many of our most endearing hymns.

"The whole Christian world sings his 'Rock of Ages.' Thousands of hearts have been melted by the hymns of Toplady. Let us be faithful witnesses, however humble our efforts may appear. Little do we know how the Spirit may use our stammering words."[3]

CHAPTER 4

The Spirit of a Servant

Clambering pell-mell over each other, multitudes of millions rush toward the object called success. Some seek to reach their destination by roughly stamping over others to get there, only to be lost in the shuffle and left wondering what went wrong. Careening crazily down the highway of life and bypassing rules in order to reach success, many have crashed and are left desolate.

Jesus Christ stated the basic truth of success when He taught His disciples how to be great: "Whosoever will be great among you, let him be your minister; and whosoever will be chief among you, let him be your servant" (Matthew 20:26-27).

That does not sound like success to some people. They cry, "To be a servant? That teaching is absurd." Yet upon closer examination it does not appear to be so crazy. Is not the great doctor but a servant to people? What about the politician or the public leader, the minister or the banker; they are servants to people. Without people their office or position would no longer exist. To serve is not so demeaning after all, but it is fulfillment. It is actually the spirit of serving that makes a person great.

There was a young man who was captured in his youth, taken by the Babylonians into the court of King Nebuchadnezzar. There he was almost slain before he had a chance in life (Daniel 2:13).

When Daniel heard that he and his fellows were to be killed at the king's command, he inquired of the captain of the king's guard as to why the decree was so hasty. Arioch, the captain, gave him the reason: the failure of the wise men to make known a dream to the king. When he heard this Daniel asked the king for more time. That night God revealed the secret to Daniel that had been troubling the king.

Immediately Daniel blessed the name of God, thanking and praising Him (Daniel 2:20, 23). Daniel revealed his spirit of thanksgiving and praise again when he stood in the presence of the king and magnified God (Daniel 2:28).

The king sensed something special about Daniel and exalted him to the position of "ruler over the whole province of Babylon, and chief of the governors over all the wise men of Babylon" (Daniel 2:48). After being promoted to this great position Daniel made a request to the king in behalf of his three friends, Shadrach, Meshach, and Abednego. He asked that they be placed in a position to oversee the affairs of the province of Babylon, and the king agreed. Because of Daniel's excellent spirit, he did not forget his friends on his way up.

We see over and over instances that reveal his spirit. When he was commanded to eat the king's meat, Daniel requested that he might not defile himself with it. He did not say, "I'm not going to do that," in a belligerent attitude, even though in his heart he knew he would not do it. Instead he was tactful and courteous.

After the deaths of Nebuchadnezzar and Belshazzar, King Darius of Persia ruled over the land. He too sensed in Daniel a special quality and made him the first president of the land and ruler over the whole realm. When jealous officials sought to find fault with him, someone spoke up, "We shall not find any occasion against this Daniel, except we find it against him concerning the law of his God" (Daniel 6:5).

Daniel 6:10 reveals the secret of his greatness. After the king's decree forbidding prayer to anyone but him for thirty days on pain of death, Daniel went into his room, "kneeled upon his knees three times a day, and prayed, and gave thanks before his God, as he did aforetime." His communion with God was as natural as breathing. It was the core of his existence.

King Darius's description of Daniel after his night in the lions' den is significant: "O Daniel, servant of the living God, is thy God, whom thou servest continually, able to deliver thee from the lions?" (Daniel 7:20). The king identified him as a faithful servant of God.

Let us notice several important points about Daniel's servant spirit.

1. He constantly blessed and thanked the Lord.
2. He was thoughtful of his friends and considered their welfare.

3. He magnified the Lord in the presence of the ungodly.
4. He prayed habitually three times a day.
5. He had an excellent spirit.
6. He served God continually.
7. He fasted often. (See Daniel 9:3; 10:2-3.)

Daniel's spiritual life reveals his power with God. He did not grumble, "Everything is going against me," but instead he praised God always.

Being a servant does not mean being a doormat, or a weak-kneed, hobbling individual. The servants of God in the Bible were full of stamina, resolution, and power. If anyone had great power and authority it was the servants of Jesus Christ. In being His servants, they became all things to all people. (See I Corinthians 9:22.) They used their power to help other people lead fuller, richer lives by introducing them to Christ and then helping to meet their physical needs as well.

What the church needs today is not to develop more programs but to follow the example of the early church in loving, caring, sharing, and giving to one another. Love will cause us to do anything necessary. It caused Jesus to hang in pain and shame when He had the power to do otherwise. Love must become the motivating factor of the church.

The other day the phone rang and I heard a voice in distress. My heart went out to this young woman. Since I was in the middle of preparing dinner, I reached over and switched off the stove, for what I was cooking needed my attention. My whole focal point at that moment was to help someone in need.

She needed ministering to, and as I was the one she had called, I needed to minister to her. I listened to her, sympathized with her, and then gave her hope of further help, for the Bible says, "Bear ye one another's burdens, and so fulfil the law of Christ" (Galatians 6:2).

When she called me back later she said, "I felt something come across over the phone. I knew I had a friend." Ministering to others is what Christianity is all about. People do not need to be judged; they need to be loved and helped. Jesus came not to condemn but to save.

A lady called the church one night sobbing, and one of the leaders asked me to talk to her. When I answered the phone my first inclination was not to talk to her, because she was a woman I had helped many times and who always seemed to fail. It had been a year since I had talked to her, but as I listened to her sob out her story— "I need God. I can't go on living this way! Please help me!"—my heart broke within me. I thought, This woman is desperate. Forget the past, she needs help now. She said, "I need prayer tonight." I asked her if she could come to the church. She had only a fourth of a tank of gas, and she had to use that to get her children from school and to go to work, so she could not come.

I said, "Well, let's pray over the phone." Did we pray! We had an old-fashioned prayer meeting right on the phone. She cried out to God, calling on the name of the Lord, and we both felt the power of the Lord minister to her aching heart. After praying, I gave her hope for her future. As I started to hang up I told her we loved her. She said, "Oh, thank you for helping me and caring. I feel so much better now."

Was it worth it? Is it worth helping people who stumble and fall often? Jesus said it was the sick who needed a physician. The blind, the lame, the brokenhearted, the captive, the sinsick—those are the ones who need ministering to. The morning ladies prayer meeting of our church has become like a hospital in the church. People know where to come when they have a need. The ladies are never too busy to minister to the down and out, the lonely, the burdened, the sick, and the fearful. It does not matter whether the need is spiritual, financial, physical, or mental, they are there to help. The spirit of the early church has gotten a hold of them, and many miracles occur daily because of the servant spirit that characterizes that meeting.

It does not matter that their names are not splashed across the news or that most people do not know what is going on, because true servanthood does not seek to have its name in neon lights. It seeks only to do the will of the Father and to glorify Christ.

Greatness is not determined by how many people know our name. If that were true Adolf Hitler, Judas, and Cain would be considered great. Greatness is determined by our character. It consists of honesty, kindness, mercy, diligence, and perserverance. It is doing a job well, giving everything our best, loving much, caring much, and helping to lift someone else's load.

I watched a nameless young man bring a load of sacks of concrete into a lumberyard. He undid all the ropes that tied it down and rolled them up easily. To me it looked difficult, but to him it was old hat. He was doing a job and doing it well. Without people like him no churches would be built, no sidewalks poured, or skyscrapers erected. He was one of many of a chain of people who make things happen.

Many great people are involved in life but their names are never known. They are like the nameless young man I watched, doing their job with a smile. But God is a good bookkeeper. He knows if we have the true spirit of a servant and are doing our best at a job given to us, serving well. He also knows if we go beyond the appointed responsibility and reach out to help those to whom we have no obligations. That is true servanthood.

Let us not seek greatness, but let us seek to be a servant of the Lord Jesus Christ. Only then will we receive fulfillment and a reward, for the whole law is bound up in loving God with all our being and loving our neighbor as ourselves. (See Matthew 22:35-40.)

"A curious bit of history is related concerning the great violinist Paganini. One night in Paris, where he was to play before a great audience, as he was tuning his violin he broke one of the strings. A wave of disappointment swept over the audience. Paganini paid no attention to it but began to play with the three remaining strings, working his thumb on another string until that also snapped.

"Again the audience was nettled, but he continued to play until a third string snapped and hung down upon the violinist's arm. The audience plainly was becoming disgusted, believing he had a poor violin.

"Quietly stepping to the front, Paganini said: 'Ladies and gentlemen, you now hear one string and Paganini.' He began to bring such wonderful music out of that one string that the audience leaned forward in the seats and strained their necks that they might hear it all.

"He sat down as the entire house wildly applauded because he had brought so much out of so little. One string and Paganini—*one surrendered soul and God*! We may feel we can offer little through which the Holy Spirit can work, but God does great things through humble material surrendered to His touch."[3]

CHAPTER 5

The Motive of a Servant

Paul, the servant, eloquently expressed the second greatest commandment that Jesus set forth in the Gospels. "For, brethren, ye have been called unto liberty; only use not liberty for an occasion to the flesh, but by love serve one another. For all the law is fulfilled in one word, even in this; Thou shalt love thy neighbour as thyself" (Galatians 5:13-14).

Some people feel that the new freedom they find in Christ puts them in a position to act as a judge on the Supreme Court. They have the exalted opinion that their word is law and no one else's opinion is to be considered. They go from sinner to judge. Now that they have been cleansed and liberated, they become so "righteous" and "holy" that they are able to criticize, backbite, and tear apart someone else who does not measure up to their law.

While their mouth speaks Christian ethics and character, under the guise of righteousness they sow discord about someone in authority. They do not have the courage to voice their objections to the one they are talking about. No, they go around stealthily doing their dirty work while all the time pretending to be holy. God has said people with such actions will not inherit the kingdom of God. "Now the works of the flesh are manifest, which are these; adultery, fornication, uncleanness, lasciviousness, idolatry, witchcraft, hatred, variance, emulations, wrath, strife, seditions, heresies, envyings, murders, drunkenness, revellings, and such like . . . they which do such things shall not inherit the kingdom of God" (Galatians 5:19-21).

It does not matter if a person keeps every other commandment but then sows discord among the church; his actions are an abomination to God. All his good is undone by the way he treats his brother. "These six things doth the LORD hate: yea, seven are an abomination unto him: a proud look, a lying tongue, and hands that shed innocent blood, an heart that deviseth wicked imaginations, feet that be swift in running to mischief, a false witness that speaketh lies, and he that soweth discord among brethren" (Proverbs 6:16-19).

A destructive critic in the church is poisonous. He self-righteously tries to get the mote out of someone's eye while he has a beam of envy and self-righteousness in his own eye. No individual should act as a judge of other people's character and motives.

If someone says he is serving others, as Galatians 5:13 commands, but allows himself to be caught up in talebearing and sowing discord, then his service is in vain. If we feel a need to discuss something questionable about someone, let us go to the Lord with the problem and make it a matter of fervent prayer. If a situation really bothers us, we can go to the person involved with love and not a blast of hate, jealousy, and harmful criticism. Jesus condemned the wrong spirit as much as or more than sinful acts themselves.

It is impossible to serve one another as Galatians 5:13 says to do when we hurt someone by a flapping, unbridled tongue, for verse 14 says serving one another is bound up in loving our neighbor as ourselves. No one likes to have people ignore him or talk bad about him. John said, in essence, Do not tell me how much you love God when you cannot even love the people you see. (See I John 4:20.) Truly religious people have genuine love for others, and they control their tongues. James 1:26 states emphatically, "If any man among you seem to be religious, and bridleth not his tongue, but deceiveth his own heart, this man's religion is vain."

Sometimes a gossiper will justify his words by saying, "Well, I'm just talking this over with my friend," or "I'm trying to save someone from being contaminated." But actually the gossiper may be casting shadows on someone's character. Many of the things people tell about another person are exaggerated. Talebearers typically have never walked in the other person's shoes and do not know the load that person carries. They are insensitive; they do not see people through the eyes of Christ but through their own haughty magnifying glasses. Jesus called such judgmental people hypocrites.

"A little boy once went home to his mother and said, 'Mother, Sister and I went out into the garden, and we were calling about, and there was some boy mocking us.'

" 'How do you mean, Johnny,' said his mother.

" 'Why,' said the child, 'I was calling out "Ho!" and this boy said "Ho!" So I said to him, "Who are you?" and he answered, "Who are you?" I said, "What is your name?" He said, "What is your name?" And I said to him, "Why don't you show yourself?" He said, "Show yourself." '

" 'So I jumped over the ditch and I went into the wood, and I could not find him, and I came back and said, "If you don't come out I will punch your head," and he said, "I will punch your head." ' "

"His mother said, 'Ah, Johnny, if you had said, "I love you," he would have said, "I love you." If you would have said, "Your voice is sweet," he would have said, "Your voice is sweet." Whatever you said to him he would have said back to you. For you see, you were hearing an echo.' "[3]

Jesus gave us the key to what we want echoed in our lives: "With what measure ye mete, it shall be measured to you again" (Matthew 7:2).

"What a mighty engine that is," someone remarked as a huge, new locomotive rushed past. "Yes, when it is on the rails," was the stationmaster's reply. On the rails, power; off the rails, destruction. It is time for the church to get on track and become the powerhouse of love it is supposed to be.

"When Charles Spurgeon was just a boy, the family had visitors to their home in Norwood. The visitors had eyes and ears for all things and observed that Charles asked his mother for some eggs from the henhouse. Mrs. Spurgeon replied, 'Yes, Charles, but you know you have to pay for them.'

"It seemed strange to the visitor that the parents should charge their own son for eggs, and the rumor started that the Spurgeons were stingy and greedy even with their own children. They sold eggs and milk from their private dairy also. Not until after the death of the great preacher was the real explanation made public. Books were found which showed all dairy sales and profits therefrom, all of which had been devoted for years to the maintenance of two elderly widows of Welsh ministers. But the cruel critics understood not."[3]

It would be wonderful if more efforts were made to help others instead of tearing others apart. A story is told about a ruler of a certain country who decided that his subjects were too selfish and had too little regard for helping others. He slipped out one night and placed a large stone in the road. The next day the king watched from his windows to see what would happen. Some teams drove around it, cursed it, and went on their way. One man berated a populace that kept no better roads but made no attempt to move the stone out of the way. Travelers came and went, avoiding the stone, but no one offered to move it. Finally the king went to the stone in broad daylight in the sight of everyone. He pushed the stone off the road, and underneath was a box filled with gold. On the box was this inscription: "For him who takes the trouble to move this stone." There was no need to point out the moral. Each person realized that if he had only thought of the good of others, he would have reaped a rich personal reward.

We should not knock down someone who is trying to work for God and do his best; rather we should encourage and pray for him. It is easy to be negative and destructive; those kinds of people are a dime a dozen. But the church needs to realize there is none righteous but God. "But we are all as an unclean thing, and all our righteousnesses are as filthy rags" (Isaiah 64:6).

"Let me wash your feet" should characterize our spirit, instead of "Let me tar and feather you." Paul coupled serving one another and loving one's neighbor; he did not separate them. It is impossible to speak evil of one's neighbor to someone else and love that neighbor at the same time. If a person smiles at someone he undermines, bids him good day, maybe gives him a gift, and partakes of his food, he is not "serving one another." He is slicing one another! If someone has surgery knives out waiting to pounce on the next victim, yet he smiles and acts as if everything is all right to that person's face, his actions are revolting to God.

It is possible for someone to become so busy tearing down others, afraid they are going to get ahead, that he cannot see what God wants to do. The eye follows those who are under attack, waiting for them to make a mistake, so he can pounce on it and say as in Psalm 70:3, "Aha, aha," almost rejoicing in their wrongs instead of praying and believing in them. That is not a servant spirit; that is a judging spirit.

After Jesus proclaimed, "He that is greatest among you shall be your servant" (Matthew 23:11), He immediately denounced the haughty spirit of the Pharisees of His day. He said they were "whited sepulchres, which indeed appear beautiful outward, but are within full of dead men's bones, and of all uncleanness. Even so ye also outwardly appear righteous unto men, but within ye are full of hypocrisy and iniquity. . . . Ye serpents, ye generation of vipers, how can ye escape the damnation of hell?" (Matthew 23:27-28, 33).

If all the law is fulfilled in loving our neighbor, then any action that goes against this principle is sin. It does not matter how well a person acts in another area, if he does not love his neighbor as himself, then all is lost.

If a church stops gossiping and starts praying and praising, loves instead of shoves, mortifies the flesh instead of others, that church will have revival—all because the people truly serve and love one another.

"A traveler who visited the cathedral at Pisa relates how he stood beneath its wonderful dome and gazed with awe upon its graceful proportions. Suddenly the air was filled with music. The great dome vibrated with harmony. Waves of music swelled like the roll of a great organ, then became soft, far-reaching echoes, melting into stillness in the distance.

"The harmonies had been produced by the guide who, lingering behind a moment, had softly struck a triple chord. Beneath the magic dome every sound resolves into harmony and no discord can reach the summit of the dome and live. Every voice, footstep, murmur, or bustle of the crowd is somehow blended into pleasing notes.

"If a dome, the work of man's hands, can thus harmonize all discords, can we doubt that under the great dome of God's heaven all can be made to work together for the furtherance of God's redemptive purpose toward all who love Him? Every affliction, tear, and grief will be blended into harmony within the overarching dome of divine grace."[3]

If we will seek to be kind and not be in such a rush that we blindly ignore the needs of others, we can eradicate much pain. The Samaritan took time to help a beaten man who was bleeding and helpless. Are we guilty of having the spirit of the priest and the Levite, or do we have the spirit of the man in the following account who helped a poor, worn-out soldier?

"A soldier, worn out in his country's service, sought to make a living by playing in the streets of Vienna. After a while his hand became feeble and his music was very poor. One day while he sat in great despondency, a man passed who paused and said, 'My friend, you are too feeble to play; let me take your violin.'

"He then began to play exquisite music. A great crowd gathered and coins poured in until the soldier's hat was full. 'Put those coins in your pocket,' said the violinist, 'and start over again.'

"Again the hat was filled as the violinist played more sweetly than before. Then the hearers began to whisper, 'Who is it?' Someone entering the crowd said: 'Why, that is Bucher, the famous violinist.' "[3]

Yes, the artist had taken the old soldier's place, borne his burden, played his music, and earned his livelihood. So the Lord Jesus came, bore our burden, and ascended up to glory. We His followers must help the feeble, the needy, the worn, the sick, and the torn—anyone who has a need. If we as the body of Christ will accept the challenge, the world will see Christ in us and cry, "The LORD, he is the God," as the people did on Mt. Carmel with Elijah (I Kings 18:39), for love is the loudest language of all!

CHAPTER 6

The Character of a Servant

Let us look into history at a favored child. He told his brothers that he had a dream. He said, "We were binding sheaves in the field, and, lo, my sheaf arose, and also stood upright; and, behold, your sheaves stood round about, and made obeisance to my sheaf" (Genesis 37:7).

The brothers rose up against him and said, "Shalt thou indeed reign over us? . . . And they hated him yet the more for his dreams, and for his words" (Genesis 37:8). Joseph knew their hatred but kept talking. He told them about another dream in which the sun, moon, and eleven stars bowed down to him; this made the brothers rage with envy.

Not long after his brothers went to Shechem to feed their father's flock, Jacob, the father, called his favorite son and said, "Do not thy brethren feed the flock in Shechem? come, and I will send thee unto them" (Genesis 37:13).

Amazement struck me when I read Joseph's answer. It is the first clue to the real spirit inside of him. He did not say, "There is no way I am going to go to them, for they hate me." Instead he simply answered in a *submissive* spirit, "Here am I" (Genesis 37:13).

So Joseph started walking through the vale of Hebron, and soon he came to Shechem. He wandered around looking for his brothers until a man saw him and asked what he was doing. He told him he had a message for his brothers but could not seem to find them. The man informed Joseph that he had heard them say they were going to Dothan. So to Dothan Joseph went, where he found his brothers. Before he ever reached them they were conspiring to kill him. Their sarcastic remark about him was, "Behold, this dreamer cometh" (Genesis 37:19).

Reuben intervened and offered a compromise. Instead of killing Joseph, they would just strip him of his coat and put him into a pit without any water. Sometime later the brothers saw an Ishmaelite caravan coming and decided to sell him for a slave. So Joseph was on his way to a foreign country as a slave, stripped of everything he owned. It was not a very good beginning for a ruler.

The Ishmaelites sold Joseph to Potiphar, an officer of Pharaoh in Egypt. "And the LORD was with Joseph, and he was a prosperous man; and he was in the house of his master the Egyptian. And his master saw that the LORD was with him, and that the LORD made all that he did to prosper in his hand. And Joseph found grace in his sight, and he served him" (Genesis 39:2-4).

Again we see the true spirit of greatness, the servant spirit. Joseph first served his father in a willing manner;

now he served Potiphar. The young man with all the dreams inside of him served. Nothing can keep the true servant spirit from rising. As Jesus said, to be great a person must learn to serve.

While Joseph was serving, Potiphar's wife was attracted to him and tempted him. Joseph declined her offer, and she was outraged and humiliated. Again Joseph was unjustly treated. He was thrown into a pit again. This time it was a prison.

Again Joseph served well. The keeper of the prison committed to Joseph's oversight all the prisoners. Even in prison Joseph had a place of leadership, which was the Lord's doing.

Two men had dreams while in prison and were troubled by them. Joseph asked them, "Wherefore look ye so sadly to day?" (Genesis 40:7). He could have ignored them, but his caring, servant spirit made him ask. When he heard the dreams he interpreted them. He could have kept the knowledge to himself, but he blessed them by sharing what he knew. An *unselfish* spirit was Joseph's.

Stuck in a prison away from his dreams and the limelight, Joseph was steadfast and faithful. Even in a foreign country and in a dungeon he kept his integrity. He was young and handsome but misunderstood, lied about, and envied. For two years he served without respite from his lot in life, but he kept a right spirit. Being unjustly punished and hidden from proper society, with only prisoners and rats for his social life, could make any man bitter, but Joseph served well even in adverse circumstances.

The day came when the king had a dream, and the butler remembered Joseph, the man who had interpreted his dream. Joseph was called for and again served by interpreting his dream. Because of his wisdom, the king made him ruler over all the land. He was exalted from the pit to the throne because he had learned to serve well.

The true spirit of servanthood manifested itself even when Joseph's brothers came to him for grain. He could have been vindictive, but he chose to be merciful. He was the mighty leader of Egypt. He had power to seek revenge and get even, but the sight of his family caused him to weep. He was still tender and forgiving; life's bitter trials had not caused him to become hard and calloused. He had the true character of a servant: willing, forgiving, serving, and seeking the welfare of others. One of Joseph's most prominent character traits was his eagerness to return good for evil.

Before he ever saw his brothers he had already settled the matter in his heart. The names of his two sons tell it all. "And Joseph called the name of the firstborn Manasseh [Forgetting]: For God, said he, hath made me forget all my toil, and all my father's house. And the name of the second called he Ephraim [Fruitful]: For God hath caused me to be fruitful in the land of my affliction" (Genesis 41:51-52).

What he was saying is, "I am not carrying the bitterness and bad memories of hard work and trials around with me." He did not deny his hardships, but he acknowledged the will and blessings of God in all that happened to him. He was seventeen when he first encountered bitter hatred, and for thirteen years he served well, until he was made the highest ruler in the land of Egypt under Pharoah.

The character of a servant rests deep inside a person and surfaces at every interlude of life. Whether in war or peace, in a prison or a palace, in the city or the country, true servanthood is exhibited by a great spirit. The following story illustrates this truth.

"A Russian soldier, one very cold night, kept duty between two sentry depots. A poor workingman, moved with pity, took off his coat and lent it to the soldier to keep him warm. 'I'll soon reach home,' he said to the soldier, 'but you'll be exposed all night to the bitter wind.'

"Some time afterward this workingman lay desperately sick, and the physician said there was no hope of recovery. As he neared the end, he seemed one night to see a vision. He thought he saw the Saviour. The coat He wore looked strangely familiar. 'That looks like my coat,' he said to the Master. To his great surprise the Saviour answered: 'Do you recall a very cold night when I was on sentry duty and you passed by?'

" 'I remember giving my coat to a soldier,' the man answered, 'but he did not resemble You.' And the Saviour smiled and said: 'Inasmuch as ye have done it unto the least of these my brethren, ye have done it unto me.' "[3]

Caring enough to give our coat or to wrap someone up in our love is the mark of true greatness. Selfishness and greed are the marks of the haughty, the opposite of the servant. Let us examine the years we have lived, the ways and paths our feet have trod. Have they walked down streets of love and care, or have they walked with hate and unconcern?

What gates have you opened? What gates did you pass? Did jealousy beckon to you beyond the gate, and did you walk through? Did envy and revenge bid you to come in? Did bitterness and strife offer you comfort, and did you accept?

If you did, there is still hope. You can begin anew. This is a new day, a day of fresh beginnings. You can walk out of those gates of jealousy, anger, and revenge and close them tightly behind you. Walk further down the path of life and open gates of love, kindness, and servanthood. You have the power through Christ to do so. Let the character of a true servant become a part of your whole being, for Jesus said, "He that is greatest among you shall be your servant" (Matthew 23:11).

CHAPTER 7

Servant to the Undeserving

For years I had heard Luke 6:38 quoted and used with reference to financial giving and blessing. Although the principle applies to financial giving, Jesus did not limit this remark to money: "Give, and it shall be given unto you: good measure, pressed down, and shaken together, and running over, shall men give into your bosom. For with the same measure that ye mete withal it shall be measured to you again."

Early one morning during my time with God, He opened up my understanding as to the meaning of this verse of Scripture. He had impressed me to do something very unorthodox for a group of unbelievers, and He knew that I needed some assurance that it was the right thing to do. While I was talking to Him, Luke 6 came to my mind, so I turned to that chapter and began to read. It seemed that lights began flashing in my brain, and He showed me a truth that had been there all the time but was new to me. I had read it before, but this time it stood out in bold print and leaped at me.

The lesson actually begins at Luke 6:20, but let us look particularly at verses 35-38:

> *But love ye your enemies, and do good, and lend, hoping for nothing again; and your reward shall be great, and ye shall be the children of the Highest: for he is kind unto the unthankful and to the evil. Be ye therefore merciful, as your Father also is merciful. Judge not, and ye shall not be judged: condemn not, and ye shall not be condemned: forgive, and ye shall be forgiven: give, and it shall be given unto you. . . .*

Let us notice the colon between "forgiven" and "give." Jesus was teaching about the proper attitude to unbelievers. He was not talking primarily about giving money; He was talking about giving kindness, forgiveness, and mercy.

The point that was impressed so forcibly upon me was the last phrase of verse 35: "For he is kind unto the unthankful and to the evil." He is kind not only to His followers but to the unthankful and evil.

What does it mean to be kind or show kindness? Webster says it means "1. Disposed to do and confer happiness, benevolent, sympathetic, showing tenderness, gracious. 2. Characterized by goodness, gentleness, or benevolence. Pleasant, acceptable, grateful, loving, affectionate. 3. Showing goodwill and friendship."

What would happen if all Christians treated the people

who do not know Christ with the spirit just defined? If all unbelievers, including the grouchy clerks, impatient motorists, cheating businessmen, rude consumers, prostitutes, drug addicts, and derelicts were treated in a gentle, kind, gracious, and tender manner, there would be a revival such as the early church experienced.

How can Christians who claim to be in love with Christ glare back at an angry motorist or look with disdain at a prostitute, and not feel bad about doing so? It is because we walk too much in the flesh and not in the Spirit. Why does the Christian feel as if he is better than the fallen, set himself up on a judgment seat, and point his righteous finger at sinners, when Jesus came not to condemn them but to save? Immediately after Jesus said that God is kind to the unthankful and to the evil, He instructed us to be merciful as our Father is merciful. Then He said not to condemn or judge but to forgive. He was not merely talking about another saint; he was talking about the worst sinner.

A good servant obeys his master's wishes. He does not question them, argue, or try to reason them out; he simply obeys. Instead of trying to figure out all the Master's plans, let us simply love unbelievers and be kind to them. We should go out of our way to do things for them, to woo them and win them to Christ by our kind spirit.

If you fail at times and are not kind or find yourself condemning the unbeliever, repent. Ask God to put a merciful attitude like His inside you and enable you to see people through His eyes.

If there ever was a need for kindness, it is now. The very work of the evil one is present among us with harshness, anger, impatience, ill will, suspicion, and greed.

God did not ask us to destroy people or condemn them to punishment. Christ came to seek and to save the lost (Luke 19:10), and we are to do likewise. Instead sometimes we become like the disciples in the following story. One day Jesus decided to go to Jerusalem. On his way He sent messengers ahead to make preparations for Him in a village of the Samaritans, but the village would not receive Him because He was going to Jerusalem. When James and John saw this response, they asked to consume the village with fire from heaven. But Jesus rebuked them, "Ye know not what manner of spirit ye are of. For the Son of man is not come to destroy men's lives, but to save them" (Luke 9:55-56).

Their attitude is like the little boy who overheard his friend's mother say she was going to spank her little boy. He taunted his friend, "You're going to get a whipping. You're going to get a whipping." Could it be that some Christians get a feeling of delight when an unbeliever is judged? Could they be saying with the little boy, "You're going to burn. You're going to burn"? Then do they walk away, leaving sinners in despair, wrapping their self-righteous robes around them instead of showing them the cleansing blood of Christ and His merciful love?

"There was a poor widow who made her living by taking in washing and depended greatly upon the produce from her garden. One night several boys robbed her garden and then turned some pigs into the garden so that it was ruined by morning. The widow had to suffer through the winter because of the loss of her vegetables. As she looked at the ruined garden she picked up a knife with a name engraved on the handle. The name belonged to a boy she knew.

"Later a revival took place in the town and among those who became converted was the boy whose name was on the knife. Then he went to the widow and told her he was sorry. When she told him she knew that he was involved in the trouble, he asked, 'Why didn't you report me and make me pay the damage?'

" 'There was a more excellent way,' she said. 'I began to pray that God would save your soul; then I knew you would want to make everything right.' "[3]

What a powerful witness! She definitely was paid greater dividends through her prayer than she would have been by the law. God's ways work even though they are unusual and unorthodox.

The same message about sin and its results can be delivered two different ways. When a man is sinking, he does not need a weight; he needs a lifeboat. People who are sunk in sin's mire need to hear about deliverance from the judgment that is soon to be theirs if they do not repent. The attitude with which the message is imparted will make a difference in how it is received.

Jesus was more compassionate and tender toward unbelievers than He was the Pharisees, the religious leaders of that day. He went out of His way to dine with sinners, to give them hope and help them out of their dilemmas. He violated Pharisaic traditions regarding the Sabbath in order to heal and help the needy. He set the tongues of the Pharisees wagging when He ate with sinners.

He spoke out in the synagogue about what he came to do: "The Spirit of the Lord is upon me, because he hath anointed me to preach the gospel to the poor; he hath sent me to heal the brokenhearted, to preach deliverance to the captives, and recovering of sight to the blind, to set at liberty them that are bruised" (Luke 4:18).

The people thought highly of his manner of speaking. "And all bare him witness, and wondered at the gracious words which proceeded out of his mouth" (Luke 4:22). The words were gracious because His gospel was one of love, deliverance, hope, and light. It contrasted sharply with the harshness of the hypocritical Pharisees' speech.

The purpose of Christ was to lift people up from darkness to light. Although he walked among them, He never compromised His doctrine or became tainted by their sin. He remained pure and holy, affecting His world. His gospel remained what it was, a light. That light shone on people's lives, and the blackness of their sin showed clearly. So powerful was that light and His drawing power that the worst of sinners melted in His presence, asking to be forgiven.

The powerful force of the love of Christ that emanated from the early church confounded both the religious leaders and the rankest sinners. It gave the believers boldness to declare sin and pronounce judgment upon evil while at the same time offering hope. The religious leaders were not accustomed to this power and doctrine. They were used to prisoners cursing, fighting back, becoming angry and defiant.

Gamaliel, a doctor of the law, stood up for the disciples at a time when many leaders wanted to kill them. He said, in essence, If this movement is of God, you cannot over-throw it. So instead of killing them, they only beat them. After the beating they commanded them not to teach or preach in the name of Jesus.

Let us notice the disciples' reaction. They had just been beaten, and yet their attitude was one of rejoicing. It was not one of condemnation toward their persecutors. "And they departed from the presence of the council, re-joicing that they were counted worthy to suffer shame for his name. And daily in the temple, and in every house, they ceased not to teach and preach Jesus Christ" (Acts 5:41-42).

The boldness that the gospel brought to the early church was not used to condemn men and women; it was used to reveal sin and to glorify Christ. When Paul and Barnabas were journeying through the island of Cyprus, they found a false prophet whose name was Bar-jesus. He accompanied the deputy of the country, Sergius Paulus, who was a prudent man. When the deputy saw the disciples, he called to them and asked to hear the Word of God.

As they began to speak, the sorcerer tried to turn the deputy away from the faith. Then Paul, filled with the Holy Ghost, turned to him and said, "O full of all subtilty and all mischief, thou child of the devil, thou enemy of all righteousness, wilt thou not cease to pervert the right ways of the Lord? And now, behold, the hand of the Lord is upon thee, and thou shalt be blind, not seeing the sun for a season. And immediately there fell on him a mist and a darkness; and he went about seeking some to lead him by the hand. Then the deputy, when he saw what was done, believed, being astonished at the doctrine of the Lord" (Acts 13:10-12).

God defended His gospel. A sinner was hungry for God, but Satan was working through a vessel to draw the sinner away from believing. Paul spoke with boldness to the instrument of the devil. He attacked the problem, but he did not attack the sorcerer personally. He was dealing with opposition from Satan. It was love that motivated him to deal with the problem. He had a love for the gospel of Jesus Christ, and he cared for the destiny of the deputy's soul. That love produced boldness to deal with whatever would thwart the working of the gospel, whether is be demon, carnal human, or sin.

Some people think that when we talk about love we are advocating compromise and weakness. But love is the strongest force in the world. It is powerful enough to stand against evil without compromising principles and doctrines. The opposite is true of a judgmental spirit. It breeds weakness, hate, cynicism, and harshness. Love breeds strength, power, and hope.

Kindness and mercy are not weakness. Over and over again, like a solid cable the doctrine of Christ attaches itself to the electrical current of love, mercy, and kindness. Men wanted to condemn the sinner caught in adultery, but Christ wanted to forgive. Mercy is stated in His teachings, and it is seen in His manner of handling situations. He cared more for the souls of people than He did for cold, hard reasons.

Let us examine our attitudes, asking ourselves, Do I look with disgust and loathing at the sinner? Do I return temper with temper? Do I move in my own clean, comfortable circle, or do I reach out to the man in the tree or the woman by the well? Do I present Christ in love and tenderness, or do I present Him with a finger shaking angrily in the sinner's face? Do I walk by the hurting person, or do I care enough to share? Have I been judgmental of others' weakness so I can excuse my own uncaring attitude by saying, "It's their own fault. They deserve what they got!" Do I shun the woman with five husbands, saying, "She made her bed; now she's got to lie in it"? Where are my feelings? What motivates me? Is my heart a polished veneer on the outside but corroded within? Am I sensitive enough to God to ask forgiveness for my attitude? Am I sitting on a throne, or am I kneeling in a servant's position?

My prayer today is:

Father, forgive me for my disdain,
For not being able to see the pain
Of someone who's hurting and in need,
And not being able to see when others bleed.

I ask You today to wash away callousness,
And fill me with love and kind tenderness.
Wash me clean from judgmentalism and bitterness;
Let my life be characterized by kindness.

Submissive at Your feet I kneel,
As I think of Calvary's hill,
Where You uttered those final words—
"Father, forgive them" is what they heard.

A servant's attitude, kind and true,
Let it be mine, to resemble you.
The unthankful, and those who don't deserve,
Let me with Your love and grace always serve.
Amen.

Joy Haney

"Sometime ago at Trongate, England, a touching sight was seen. An old lady with a shawl over her head, seemingly very poor, was noticed by a policeman picking up something from the roadway and hurriedly depositing it in her apron. She continued to do this as though she was finding something of value perhaps dropped by another.

"The officer, new to his duties, and a bit puffed up with his new authority, went up to the old woman and said rather gruffly: 'What is it you're hiding there in your apron? What are you up to? Open up that apron or I'll run you in.'

"The little old lady smilingly opened the apron, and there were bits of broken glass, nails, and other sharp objects gathered from the path. 'Why are you doing that?' asked the officer.

"'I just pick them up every day,' she said shyly, 'because so many barefooted children come this way every day and are liable to cut their feet.' The big policeman blushed, and putting his big arm around her shoulders, said: 'God bless you, lady!' "[3]

Humble service motivated this lady. She did not care who was watching. She did not do it for laurels, but because she loved.

CHAPTER 8

Roll Call of Servants

Everyone is a servant of someone or something. The greats of the Bible were servants to God. Many were not identified as such in so many words, but some were, as shown in the following list. Will your name join this group?

Abraham . "his servant" (Psalm 105:6)
Moses ... "my servant" (Numbers 12:7)
Caleb .... "my servant" (Numbers 14:24)
Daniel ... "servant of the living God" (Daniel 6:20)
David .... "my servant" (I Kings 11:34)
Nehemiah "thy servant" (Nehemiah 1:11)
Isaiah.... "my servant" (Isaiah 20:3)
Job ...... "my servant" (Job 1:8)
Peter .... "a servant ... of Jesus Christ" (II Peter 1:1)
Phoebe... "a servant of the church" (Romans 16:1)
Jude ..... "servant of Jesus Christ" (Jude 1)

James ... "a servant of God" (James 1:1)
Anna .... "served God" (Luke 2:37)
Paul ..... "a servant of Jesus Christ" (Romans 1:1)

Sometimes Christians feel that they should get first-class service for themselves and not share the workload of the kingdom. In other words, they would rather be waited on than wait on others. The following story says it well.

"In the days of the stagecoach, a man undertook a journey. He was informed that there were first-, second-, and third-class passengers. However, all the seats on the coach looked alike to him, so he purchased a third-class ticket. All went well for a time, and the man was congratulating himself upon having saved some money.

"Presently they came to the foot of a very steep hill, when the driver stopped the horses and shouted, 'First-class passengers keep your seats, second-class get out and walk, third-class get out and push behind.'

"What we need in the kingdom work is third-class passengers. Those who will push! Not first-class, who are contented to sit and look on while others are working, but third-class passengers who are willing to bear the burden and heat of the day."[4]

We are all first class with God, but we are all expected to work for Him. It does not matter what our name is or who our parents were, the thing that matters to Him is whether we are willing to be a servant of the Lord Jesus Christ.

Position is not important; attitude is the most important thing. It is not our clothes, house, car, or circle of friends that counts but our motives, spirit, and character.

Servanthood is not for the arrogant and the lazy; it is for men and women who are willing to work, hurt, and give. One of the greatest servants of God, who is probably quoted more than any other servant, suffered more than most people comprehend. He is quoted, honored, and highly esteemed, but who wants to walk the road he walked to get there?

Before his servanthood to Christ, he was a servant to a system. He was educated at Jerusalem in the school of Gamaliel. He was an arrogant Pharisee who persecuted Christians. But his true service to God began on the road to Damascus, where he was struck down by a powerful light that blinded him. After hearing God speak to him, he was baptized, filled with the Spirit, and called to be an apostle.

What a road he traveled after that encounter! He first preached in Damascus and was persecuted by the Jews there (Acts 9:23-24). He escaped by being let down over the city wall in a basket. He went to Arabia, Jerusalem, Caesarea, and Tarsus. Eventually Barnabas brought him to Antioch, and they taught there together for one year (Acts 11:26). From there Paul and Barnabas were sent as missionaries to the Gentiles (Acts 13:1-4).

Paul's life became a whirlwind. His first missionary journey began with a visit to Seleucia and Cyprus. From there he went to Perga in Pamphylia and to Antioch in Pisidia. The Gentiles there received his message gladly.

The Jews did not like this, for they were filled with envy (Acts 13:45), so they persecuted Paul and Barnabas and expelled them from the city. From there the missionaries went to Iconium. They preached there but were persecuted, so again they fled for their lives and went to Lystra and Derbe. In Lystra, Paul healed a lame man through the power of God, but eventually he faced persecution again and was stoned. The people dragged him out of the city and left him for dead (Acts 14:19).

A bystander might have exclaimed after watching Paul for a while, "The life of a servant is dangerous, the wages are lousy, and the reception is uncertain! Who wants to live that kind of life?"

Paul, who was on fire with his message, would have answered him like this:

None of these things move me, neither count I my life dear unto myself (Acts 20:24).

For though I be free from all men, yet have I made myself servant unto all (I Corinthians 9:19).

Who shall separate us from the love of Christ? shall tribulation, or distress, or persecution, or famine, or nakedness, or peril, or sword? . . . Nay, in all these things we are more than conquerors through him that loved us (Romans 8:35, 37).

We are troubled on every side, yet not distressed; we are perplexed, but not in despair; persecuted, but not forsaken; cast down, but not destroyed; always bearing about in the body the dying of the Lord Jesus, that the life also of Jesus might be made manifest in our body (II Corinthians 4:8-10).

Therefore I take pleasure in infirmities, in reproaches, in necessities, in persecutions, in distresses for Christ's sake: for when I am weak, then am I strong (II Corinthians 12:10).

For I know whom I have believed, and am persuaded that he is able to keep that which I have committed unto him against that day (II Timothy 1:12).

The key to Paul's success in serving God appears in the last sentence: "I have committed." Servanthood is commitment. He became a servant to the core; nothing could shake him. He had a conviction.

Was Paul a superhero? No, he was as fleshly as any man or woman. He felt the stones, and they hurt. The beatings did not fall upon glorified flesh. His back hurt as much as anyone else's would have. How then could he change so suddenly from being the persecutor to the one persecuted?

He summed it all up by saying, "For the love of Christ constraineth us. . . . Therefore if any man be in Christ, he is a new creature" (II Corinthians 5:14, 17). The new love that was born in his heart captivated and changed him. He used the verb *constrain*, which means to compel, coerce, push, or drive. It was not always easy for Paul to suffer the things he did as a result of being a servant, but the love he had for Christ compelled him to endure it with joy. The love was bigger than the pain. It was his first priority. As a shoemaker once said, "I serve God, and make boots in my spare time."

CHAPTER 9

Addicted to Serving

Addiction means to be controlled by something or entirely given over to a practice or habit. People who are addicted to drugs are pathetic, and their plight is heart-wrenching, but there was a man in the Bible who was addicted to something good. His lifestyle ruled his addiction.

Paul described this man and family in these words: "Ye know the house of Stephanas, that it is the firstfruits of Achaia, and that they have addicted themselves to the ministry of the saints" (I Corinthians 16:15). He continued in verses 17-18, "That which was lacking . . . they have supplied. For they have refreshed my spirit and yours."

Such people are a breath of fresh air. Instead of always demanding, "Give me," they say, "Let me help" and "What can I do for you?" The most blessed people are the ones who give themselves to a higher cause that blesses others. (See Acts 20:35.)

In fact, judgment comes on those who do the opposite. In Deuteronomy 23:4, God pronounced a curse upon the Moabites because they did not give bread and water to the Israelites when they came out of Egypt. God shut up their blessing when they shut up the supply line to the needy.

Jesus said, "I am the bread of life" (John 6:35). We must give the world spiritual bread and minister to their physical needs as well.

"For God is not unrighteous to forget your work and labour of love, which ye have shewed toward his name, in that ye have ministered to the saints, and do minister" (Hebrews 6:10). We show our love to God when we care for each other. God is keeping records; if we give someone a cup of water in His name, we will be rewarded, for we have done it to Him (Mark 9:41).

Addiction to ministry or service has to be more than just praying for people. It goes further than that. "What doth it profit, my brethren, though a man say he hath faith, and have not works? can faith save him? If a brother or sister be naked, and destitute of daily food, and one of you say unto them, Depart in peace, be ye warmed and filled; notwithstanding ye give them not those things which are needful to the body, what doth it profit?" (James 2:14-16).

For example, a lady asked for prayer in our ladies prayer meeting. She needed $167.85 for a utility bill, and because of hard times, did not have the money to pay it. Service was going to be cut off within forty-eight hours.

We prayed. While praying, several ladies felt impressed to take up an offering for her. We each expressed how we felt and then proceeded to receive a free-will love offering. When the money was counted, the total amount was $167.00, and then a lady went up and handed her a handful of change. We praised and glorified God for the miracle and left there feeling terrific.

"As we have therefore opportunity, let us do good unto all men, especially unto them who are of the household of faith" (Galatians 6:10).

The ladies who have been involved in these "opportunities," which have come quite often, are joyously and gloriously blessed. They have a song and excitement about them. Not only is God blessing them spiritually, but He is blessing them in the natural. His system works! If we want to be happy we should follow these instructions: "Charge them that are rich in this world . . . that they do good, that they be rich in good works, ready to distribute, willing to communicate [share]" (I Timothy 6:17-18).

I had an opportunity to go to Egypt in 1987, and when I got off the tour bus, immediately a group of young Egyptian girls surrounded me and reached out to touch me. They kept saying, "Rich American." I saw a lot of poverty there and realized that even those who consider themselves to be having a hard time in America are rich compared to many people in other countries.

It is an easy thing to give of our abundance but harder for us to give if sacrifice is involved; nevertheless, giving is God's way. It is also the way to be blessed. My husband tells about a Bible school his father attended in Oakland, California, run by Harry Morris in 1935. Every time the school did not have enough food to feed the students, he would take an offering for the missionaries, and God would always send the food they needed.

The law of Christ is actually fulfilled when we care enough to share and care about another's lack. "Bear ye one another's burdens, and so fulfil the law of Christ" (Galatians 6:2). The second of the two commandments upon which the whole law hinges is, "Love thy neighbour as thyself" (Matthew 22:39-40). "By love serve one another" (Galatians 5:13).

Loving service was part of Paul's lifestyle. On one occasion he said, "I go unto Jerusalem to minister unto the saints. For it hath pleased them of Macedonia and Achaia to make a certain contribution for the poor saints which are at Jerusalem" (Romans 15:25-26).

Addiction eats at a person. The addict craves what he is addicted to. Addiction has a hold on him with a tenacious grip. It is his lord and master. It becomes the controlling force in his life. Stephanas was addicted to the ministry of the saints. He was known as a giver.

If you are leery about giving to other people, afraid you are going to be cheated or deceived, then simply give on the authority of the Word of God and in the name of Jesus. "And whatsoever ye do in word or deed, do all in the name of the Lord Jesus" (Colossians 3:17).

When we have given all we feel we can give and we have influence on others who are more blessed to give, then we can go to them in behalf of the ministry of the saints. We must first provide for the needs of our family, but we are also instructed to give to others. God will give us the wisdom to know what to give and how much to give, if we trust Him and listen carefully to His direction. He expects us to be good stewards of our time and money.

Love will make a way. Jesus taught, "Love one another; as I have loved you, . . . ye also love one another. By this shall all men know that ye are my disciples, if ye have love one to another" (John 13:34-35). Three times in two verses He stressed love one for another.

"But whoso hath this world's good, and seeth his brother have need, and shutteth up his bowels of compassion from him, how dwelleth the love of God in him? My little children, let us not love in word, neither in tongue; but in deed and in truth" (I John 3:17-18). Love expresses itself in some kind of action. Love is not deaf, dumb, or blind. It sees needs and fills them. It touches, caresses, and fulfills. It listens and is sensitive.

What would happen if all who call themselves Christians really loved in this manner? They would revolutionize the world. Selfishness and greed would flee, and compassion would reign. The church would be compassionate, tender, and responsive. The little boy was not far wrong when, in comparing the love of his companions to the love of God, he exclaimed, "God is nicer'n peoples!"

Can we feel the throb in the voice of Jesus as He emphasized the importance of loving one another? Let us join Stephanas in being addicted to loving and serving. We please God greatly when we fulfill the two most important laws: loving Him with all our being and loving our neighbor as ourselves. The question pulsates in the air: how much do we really love Him?

CHAPTER 10

The Mind of a Servant

From a damp prison, Paul wrote:

Let this mind be in you, which was also in Christ Jesus: who, being in the form of God, thought it not robbery to be equal with God: but made himself of no reputation, and took upon him the form of a servant, and was made in the likeness of men: and being found in fashion as a man, he humbled himself, and became obedient unto death, even the death of the cross (Philippians 2:5-8).

Let us notice three key words: *mind, servant, humbled*. We should have the mind of a servant, which includes humility. "Humble yourselves in the sight of the Lord, and he shall lift you up" (James 4:10). One writer said a humble person recognizes that he is neither worm nor wonder. Humility is acknowledging God's greatness and being submissive to His dealings or will. The words "Let this mind be in you, which was also in Christ Jesus" need to penetrate our quest for success. They need to dominate our thoughts and actions if we want to acquire true greatness. Any form of "greatness" without humility and service is shallow.

Some people are so busy planning how to reach a place at the right hand of God, or an exalted position, that they cannot be bothered with lowly service. But the very thing they shun is what would exalt them. "For whosoever exalteth himself shall be abased; and he that humbleth himself shall be exalted" (Luke 14:11).

The question was asked about David, "Is not this David, the servant of Saul the king of Israel?" (I Samuel 29:3). He was first a servant before he was a king. He had the attitude of a servant as a shepherd for his father, and then he served the army and the king by risking his own life.

How can we serve? In many ways! True serving is motivated by a fundamental love for people, not by the attitude of "What am I going to get out of it?" Henry Ford stated, "A little bit of myself goes into every automobile that rolls off our assembly lines, and I think of every automobile we sell not in terms of profit yielded us, but in terms of useful service it may render the purchaser."

Service is determined by what controls the mind, for the mind controls all that we do. "Put on therefore, as the elect of God, holy and beloved, bowels of mercies, kindness, humbleness of mind, meekness, longsuffering" (Colossians 3:12). Instead of merely dealing with the symptoms of selfishness and jealousy, our minds need to be cleansed of the root of the problem. It does little good to run a lawnmower over weeds, for soon they will grow up again. They have to be dug out with a spade. Work is involved, but that is the only way to get rid of the roots. The grass will be greener and more productive, just as a life will be more profitable if there is a true heart searching instead of a cover-up.

In our quest for true success in God, our flesh will seek to dominate, but our spirit must learn to control the natural man. Jesus said, "I am meek and lowly" (Matthew 11:29).

Theophylact explained, "The meek are not those who are never at all angry, for such are insensible; but those who, feeling anger, control it, and are angry only when they ought to be. Meekness excludes revenge, irritability, morbid sensitiveness, but not self-defense, or a quiet steady maintenance of right." Paul wrote, "Be ye angry, and sin not" (Ephesians 4:26).

The minds of true servants are not insipid but strong. Servants of Jesus Christ are kind, caring, humble, and fair; but on the other hand they are full of fire and power. They can identify with Caleb, a servant who was strong: "But my servant Caleb, because he had another spirit with him, and hath followed me fully, him will I bring into the land whereinto he went; and his seed shall possess it" (Numbers 14:24).

Caleb followed the Lord fully. And Caleb had a different attitude than most people. True servants are different. They are not made from the same mold as the crowd; they have allowed God to shape them in a positive mold.

According to Numbers 13, the Lord commanded Moses to send men to spy out the land of Canaan, which He had promised to the Israelites. In obedience Moses sent twelve leaders representing the twelve tribes. The Bible calls them "heads" of the people.

The men left and were gone for forty days. Returning tired and worn, they told of the glories of the land, but ten of them ruined the report by saying, "Nevertheless the people be strong that dwell in the land, and the cities are walled, and very great; and moreover we saw the children of Anak there" (Numbers 13:28). They were leaders but not true servants, because to have God's mind is to have faith and power, not fear. (See II Timothy 1:7.)

The more the ten talked the bigger their fear became. As they described the rest of the obstacles, all of their remaining reasons for their fear were the people they saw. They named them all: the Amalekites in the south, the Hittites, the Jebusites, the Amorites in the mountains, and the Canaanites by the sea and Jordan. They forgot how God parted the Red Sea when the Egyptians pursued them, how He made water surge forth out of a rock for them, and how He rained food from heaven for them.

In the midst of the clamor of unbelief, there sounded a voice of authority that stilled the people. The voice that spoke was none other than Caleb, and God was pleased. Caleb said, "Let us go up at once, and possess it; for we are well able to overcome it" (Numbers 13:30). This was the spirit that God noted later. It was a complete, unreserved trust in God.

What kind of mind do we harbor in our lives? Is it a mind of humility, but strength; a total, unreserved commitment to Jesus Christ? Or is it one of pride, jealousy, and noncommitment? If the latter, let us get out the vacuum of God's Word and start doing some mind cleaning. Let us sweep out anything that exalts itself against the knowledge of God.

To have the mind of Christ is to be dominated by His thoughts and concepts. They must live, breathe, and pulsate within our hearts and minds. Instead of getting even, we need to burn with kindness. As II Corinthians 10:5 says, "Casting down imaginations, and every high thing that exalteth itself against the knowledge of God, and bringing into captivity every thought to the obedience of Christ."

Let us imagine a large, well-equipped, and well-run fruit-canning factory with an assembly line. As each worker does what he has been hired to do, he observes everyone else doing the same thing. He may think, Who set this system up? Who tells us what to do?

The president of the company has carefully designed a plan to get maximum performance out of his workers. He wants his company to be successful and productive. He knows things that the workers do not know. The company is run according to his thoughts and ideas. He is not going to work against himself; therefore, he buys and maintains the best equipment. Everything is run with precision and a plan.

The same is true with Jesus Christ. We are under His authority. We are not free to operate any way we feel, but He has given thoughts, commandments, and guidelines for us to follow. He wants only the best for His workers. His organization has the most powerful equipment to help produce the most glorious products.

We work with Him in producing love, joy, peace, longsuffering, gentleness, goodness, faith, meekness, and temperance. He does not just place the finished product in our hands. It is a process of choosing, culling, eliminating, and retaining. He gives us many instructions, such as cleanse yourselves, come out from among them, do good to those who hate you, love your enemies, and bless those who curse you. (See Matthew 5:44; II Corinthians 6:17-7:1.)

The Lord tells us what to do because He knows the weakness of our flesh. The president of the company cannot produce the fruit properly packaged without the workers' assistance, and neither does Jesus work in us without our consent and help. We are workers together with Him.

In both production plants the workers operate according to the leader's thoughts, concepts, and understanding. They are his servants in all reality. They are not free to do things their way or operate with some new idea.

Of course, in Jesus we can grow, become, and reach our potential, but even in our growth and fulfillment of dreams, we still must operate within the framework of His concepts. But what is wrong with that? "For in him we live, and move, and have our being" (Acts 17:28). It is a glorious place to be!

In all our growth, in reality it is Jesus being formed inside of us. Paul called the Galatians "my little children, of whom I travail in birth again until Christ be formed in you" (Galatians 4:19). We must disregard our old ways. Gradually we shed our ideologies as a snake sheds his skin. We put off the old man and put on the new.

Sometimes we need to stop and empty our mind of preconceived ideas, busy thoughts, confusion, and unrest. It is time to take orders from above, because God does not give confusion. He gives direction and wisdom. "The steps of a good man are ordered by the LORD" (Psalm 37:23). "Trust in the LORD with all thine heart; and lean not unto thine own understanding. In all thy ways acknowledge him, and he shall direct thy paths" (Proverbs 3:5-6).

By filling our minds with God's Word, we will be successful and fulfilled. "The righteous shall inherit the land. . . . The mouth of the righteous speaketh wisdom. . . . The law of his God is in his heart; none of his steps shall slide" (Psalm 37:29-31). His heart is no longer his; it is controlled by the law of God. He operates under a different set of rules than the average person.

Having the mind of Christ to guide us is the way to victory. His thoughts are above our thoughts. "For my thoughts are not your thoughts, neither are your ways my ways, saith the LORD. For as the heavens are higher than the earth, so are my ways higher than your ways, and my thoughts than your thoughts" (Isaiah 55:8-9).

Not everyone accepts God's way. Belligerent, bellowing fools reject His way; only the meek accept his way. "The way of a fool is right in his own eyes" (Proverbs 12:15). "The meek will he teach his way" (Psalm 25:9). God reveals secrets of wisdom to those who walk in His way and diligently seek to live under His influence.

When we were children we loved to be told secrets—those special hidden things. Spiritually speaking, we no longer have to walk in the dark; we can know the secrets too. "The secret of the LORD is with them that fear him; and he will shew them his covenant" (Psalm 25:14).

Now is the time to fear Him and think upon His name and His Word. "Then they that feared the LORD spake often one to another: and the LORD hearkened and heard it, and a book of remembrance was written before him for them that feared the LORD, and that thought upon his name" (Malachi 3:16).

When we live on this level and God tells us to do something, we do not think it strange, because we have become dead to our old ways and thoughts. If we need water and He tells us to dig ditches to get it, we dig the ditches. He then fills them His own way without wind or rain. And it is but a light thing for Him to do so. (See II Kings 3:15-18.)

Our thoughts will not be rooted in common knowledge or analysis. They will not be earthbound, but they will soar in the heavenlies. They will fly higher than the eagles. True humility is ceasing to hang onto self and releasing our heart, soul, mind, and body to Jesus Christ. This is freedom! Submission to Him—kneeling, worshiping, and unparalleled giving—is actually what liberates us.

As the company president says, "Do it this way, and you will get your paycheck and be blessed," so the Word of God says, "Let this mind be in you, which was also in Christ Jesus." He may have looked defeated at times, but He ascended into glory, just as we will eventually. Our blessings are now and future. We win all the way around.

Let us not argue with Him, but just do what He says, and our lives will flow with His blessing and His presence.

The journey of a thousand miles begins with the first step. His way may seem hard and long, but every step we take blossoms into greater joy. Owners of new puppies have their trials, new shoes have their discomforts, and a new classroom causes butterflies in the stomach. If having the mind of Christ seems foreign or new, the discomfort will pass. As we become acquainted with His direction never again will we want to go back to the old way. His way is much more superior!

Wherever you are in the journey, never go back! It is forward all the way. Take the first step or keep walking even though you may be in a valley. The high places will come. "It is God that girdeth me with strength, and maketh my way perfect. He maketh my feet like hinds' feet, and setteth me upon my high places" (Psalm 18:32-33).

"A workman visiting a large asylum near Glasgow was accosted by one of the patients with, 'Young man, did you ever thank God for your reason?' Awestruck, he answered, 'No.' 'Then do it now, for I have lost mine,' came the sermonic reply."[1]

As you read, stop and thank God for the mind that you have and ask Him to be in charge of your thoughts. Invite Him to be Lord of your life and to cleanse your mind of anything that would keep you from doing the will of the Father.

May our minds be so controlled by the Holy Spirit that we will affect our world as D. L. Moody affected the clients of a barbershop:

"Dr. Woodrow Wilson, the President of the United States, has given an interesting impression of his contact with D. L. Moody. 'I was in a barber's shop, sitting in a chair, when I became aware that a personality had entered the room. A man had come quietly in upon the same errand as myself, and sat in the next chair to me.

" 'Every word that he uttered showed a personal and vital interest in the man who was serving him; and before I got through with what was being done to me, I was aware that I had attended an evangelistic service, because Mr. Moody was in the next chair.

" 'I purposely lingered in the room after he left, and noted the singular effect his visit had upon the barbers in that shop. They talked in undertones. They did not know his name, but they knew that something had elevated their thought. And I felt that I left that place as I should have left a place of worship.' "[1]

Oh, that every Christian would have that kind of effect upon the world! It is time for our minds to be renewed daily by sitting in God's presence and reading His Word. It is time to become saturated with Him and His holiness. "Let this mind be in you, which was also in Christ Jesus."

CHAPTER 11

The Cost of Servanthood

Nicodemus had prestige, Paul had power, Zacchaeus had social status, Lydia had hospitality, but what did Mary have? She did not have much to offer, but she did have some costly ointment. Everyone gave of his substance in his own way, but they did not think of anointing Jesus—except for Mary.

She loved Him so much that she gave her most precious possession. She did not give in a cold, haughty manner but took on the form of a servant—washing His feet with costly ointment and then drying them with her hair. (See John 12.)

The greatest servant gives his best to the one he serves. He holds nothing back but works tirelessly to please. And the one who loves most, serves most.

The relationship between God and His people is a loving one. When a scribe asked Jesus what the greatest commandment was, Jesus simply answered that the first commandment was to love God with all the heart, soul, mind, and strength (Mark 12:28-30). He who loved so much that He gave expects us to love with the same feeling. He does not ask of us any more than He asked of Himself.

Love costs something. God does not want merely part of us. He does not want our leftovers, but He wants all of us.

When people were depositing money into the Temple treasury, Jesus told his disciples to notice a truth: "Many that were rich cast in much," but when the little widow put her two mites in, Jesus said, "This poor widow hath cast more in, than all . . . for all they did cast in of their abundance; but she of her want did cast in all that she had, even all her living" (Mark 12:41-44).

Her giving cost her something. Love cannot always be measured in the abundance of a gift, but in what it costs the giver. Mary gave her alabaster. Jesus gave His life. The widow gave all she had. Often the value of a gift is determined by the degree of sacrifice.

When David bought a threshing floor from Araunah to use as a place of worship, Araunah first offered to give it to him, but he refused it. "And the king said unto Araunah, Nay; but I will surely buy it of thee at a price: neither will I offer burnt offerings unto the LORD my God of that which doth cost me nothing" (II Samuel 24:24). David did not want to use something that did not cost him anything, for he knew God wanted a sacrifice.

We "are bought with a price" (I Corinthians 7:23). A cost was involved to redeem us, just as there is cost involved in our service. "The Son of man came not to be ministered unto, but to minister, and to give his life a ransom for many" (Mark 10:45).

Everyone has some ointment. Let us not hoard it, but pour it on the Lord's feet as Mary did. We can serve the Lord today by serving His body, the church.

Paul explained the cost of servanthood for him: "I am . . . in labours more abundant, in stripes above measure, in prisons more frequent, in deaths oft. Of the Jews five times received I forty stripes save one. Thrice was I beaten with rods, once was I stoned, thrice I suffered shipwreck, a night and a day I have been in the deep; in journeyings often, in perils of waters, in perils of robbers, in perils by mine own countrymen, in perils by the heathen, in perils in the city, in perils in the wilderness, in perils in the sea, in perils among false brethren; in weariness and painfulness, in watchings often, in hunger and thirst, in fastings often, in cold and nakedness. Beside those things that are without, that which cometh upon me daily, the care of all the churches" (II Corinthians 11:23-28).

Serving is not looking out for number one. It is not seeking easy roads or shunning responsibility to the hungry and needy. Doing the will of the Father is a great thing, but it can be a lonely experience at times. It can make a person harassed, distressed, and exhausted.

When we feel this way, we must withdraw and restore ourselves just as Jesus did. "And he withdrew himself into the wilderness, and prayed" (Luke 5:16). This incident took place right after He performed great miracles and ministered to multitudes.

Jesus does not want us to have permanent burnout, disillusionment, or bitterness. He wants us to give our all, but He also wants us to take time to withdraw when we feel resentment or too much pressure.

On another occasion Jesus hid Himself so no one could find Him, but they eventually did (Mark 7:24). At least He had a little respite from His responsibilities. He was not only God but also man, so He felt the same pressure we feel when we are stretched too thin.

Jesus said, "If any man come to me, and hate not his father, and mother, and wife, and children, and brethren, and sisters, yea, and his own life also, he cannot be my disciple. And whosoever doth not bear his cross, and come after me, cannot be my disciple" (Luke 14:26-27). He did not mean for us to despise our relatives or do harm to them. He did not mean for us to stand in front of a car and be killed. He simply meant that He is to be first in our lives. He has to reign supreme. He will not play second fiddle to anyone or anything.

He wants our love, dreams, will, ambitions, and motives to be nailed to the cross. We do not have to die physically on a cross—He did that for us—but we do have to pay the cost of discipleship. To be a disciple means that our allegiance is to the Master. We operate under His orders and His requirements.

One night in 1988, the Lord gave me a vivid dream. It was so powerful that I awoke trembling at His presence. I jumped out of bed, got my Bible, and went to my little study room. Immediately the Lord brought Genesis 24 to my mind. I turned to it and upon reading it fell on the floor sobbing as the Lord spoke to me.

In my dream I saw a large throne lifted up high with the Lord sitting on it. On either side were hundreds and hundreds of angels forming a line, and everything was bathed in golden light. The aisle between the two lines of angels was empty except for me. I was approaching the throne, and the angels were chanting, "An oath, an oath, you've got to take an oath." They kept repeating this until I awakened.

As I read the account of Abraham calling his servant to bring back a bride for his son, Isaac, I sobbed, "Lord Jesus, I'll take an oath. I am your servant. I will go to help bring a bride to you."

Now when I leave my family for three days to minister to ladies across America, with tears filling my eyes and a homesickness enveloping me at times, I remind myself of my servant's oath.

Pledges to the Lord do not come without weariness, pain, perils of death, loneliness, frustrations, and sometimes being misunderstood. They will lead us into unfamiliar, uncomfortable, and difficult places, but as Abraham promised his servant, "He shall send his angel before thee" (Genesis 24:7), so the Lord promises angels to minister to His children (Hebrews 1:14).

When we measure all the discomforts up to the sacrifice of the Cross, they pale into nothingness. When measured up against Paul, our fellow laborer, somehow the difficulties do not seem quite so bad.

The servant spirit must get hold of the modern-day church. The Old Testament made provision for a servant who was set free but who said, "I love my master, my wife, and my children; I will not go out free" (Exodus

21:5). At the end of six years of service, he was entitled to be released, but if he chose, he could remain a servant. In front of a judge, his master would pierce his ear with an awl to signify that he would still be a servant. This was the highest honor a servant could bestow on his master. He was no longer just a hired servant, but now he was a love servant.

The service of love is not burdensome, but it is secure and lasting. Cost means nothing, because there is love. "Then took Mary a pound of ointment of spikenard, very costly, and anointed the feet of Jesus, and wiped his feet with her hair" (John 12:3). She did not even consider cost; she only knew that she loved. This is the level of service the Master desires of His children.

We must be seized by the urgency of the hour. We must plan our strategy—plan our work and work our plan. Let us forget the cost! Let us give because we love Him and care about His purpose. Let us get on fire with it and become addicted to carrying out His desires.

Let God work through you. Give your best wherever He places you and in whatever you are doing. Be His servant everywhere, not just in the church building. Everywhere you go, be His light. Make a consecration like the young girl in the following poem did:

"I'm free, I'm free!" the young girl exclaimed,
"Free to do, free to speak, free to go, and free to claim
All that is mine. I'll heap it unto me.
I will become rich in things and liberty."

But as she looked back at the Cross that had freed her,
Her eyes filled with tears and her world began to blur;
For she saw Jesus, the One who had willingly suffered,
And as she stood gazing, it seemed that she heard . . .

Floating down through the ages, the old familiar strain:
"Take up thy cross, follow Me, and then you will really
gain."
All that had seemed important began to slip away
As she made her decision that very day.

Everything she had, she laid it down before Him,
And said, "You're my Master. With love fill me to the
brim.
Into the marketplace, on the job, gladly I will bear Your
mark
So all the world can see Your love; a light I'll be in the dark.

"I'm a servant, not forced to do so, but I give my life to You.
You'll be my guiding star in the midst of whatever I do.
I'll take on Your name, Your customs, and Your ways;
And through me, You will shine like a glorious sun ray!"

Joy Haney

Paul said in Romans, "I beseech you therefore, brethren, by the mercies of God, that ye present your bodies a living sacrifice, holy, acceptable unto God, which is your reasonable service" (Romans 12:1). He called our sacrifice a reasonable service.

Jesus said much the same in Luke 17. He asked the people what they would do if they had a servant plowing in the field and it came time to eat. Would the master tell the servant to go and eat? No, he would tell the servant to serve him first, and then he could eat. Would he thank him for serving him? No, because he did the things that were commanded him. Jesus concluded, "So likewise ye, when ye shall have done all those things which are commanded you, say, We are unprofitable servants: we have done that which was our duty to do" (Luke 17:10).

We do not think much of duty when we are love slaves to Jesus Christ; we feel privileged to work in His service. To be owned by Him, commanded by Him, to be in His presence and associated with Him is the highest honor.

David Livingstone explained it well: "People talk of the sacrifice I have made in spending so much of my life in Africa. Can that be called a sacrifice which is simply paid back as a small part of the great debt owing to our God, which we can never repay? Is that a sacrifice which brings its own reward of healthful activity, the consciousness of doing good, peace of mind, and a bright hope of a glorious destiny hereafter? Away with such a word, such a view, and such a thought! It is emphatically no sacrifice. Say rather it is a privilege."[4]

CHAPTER 12

The Reward of the Servant

The reward should not be our primary reason for serving. The thought "What am I going to get out of this?" should not be the priority of a servant. Yet Scripture does promise rewards for service. Let us consider them.

1. *Joy*. This reward is promised now, not just at a later date. For example, as we comfort others we receive joy. (See II Corinthians 7:4-7, 13.) Nothing can put a smile on one's face quicker than reaching out and helping another person in need. It is a feeling inside that cannot be measured in dollars and cents.

2. *Friendship with God*. In John 15, Jesus told us to abide in Him, continue in His love, keep His commandments, and love one another. The greatest love, He said, would be to give one's life for a friend. He could say this because He knew He would actually do it. In other words,

sometimes we must give to each other even when it hurts, but the rewards will come back a hundredfold. Jesus then said, "Henceforth I call you not servants; . . . but I have called you friends" (John 15:15).

3. *Honor from God.* "If any man serve me, let him follow me; and where I am, there shall also my servant be: if any man serve me, him will my Father honour" (John 12:26). "Humble yourselves therefore under the mighty hand of God, that he may exalt you in due time" (I Peter 5:6). By humbling herself Abigail became queen (I Samuel 25:23, 41-42).

4. *Promotion.* This goes along with honor. Many servants of God received promotions in the Scripture. God called Joseph and Daniel His servants, and both of them because of a humble attitude were elevated to higher positions in the kingdom where they lived. They both became second in command to the king.

5. *Loyalty of those we serve.* "And king Rehoboam consulted with the old men, that stood before Solomon his father while he yet lived, and said, How do ye advise that I may answer this people? And they spake unto him, saying, If thou wilt be a servant unto this people this day, and wilt serve them, and answer them, and speak good words to them, then they will be thy servants for ever" (I Kings 12:6-7). This principle works. A leader who cares about his followers will have their loyalty, not just their obedience.

6. *Confidence in our election.* "But thou, Israel, art my servant, Jacob whom I have chosen. . . . Thou whom I have taken from the ends of the earth, and called thee from the chief men thereof, and said unto thee, Thou art

my servant; I have chosen thee, and not cast thee away. Fear thou not; for I am with thee: be not dismayed: for I am thy God: I will strengthen thee; yea, I will help thee; yea, I will uphold thee with the right hand of my righteousness" (Isaiah 41:8-10). God chooses upholds, helps, and strengthens His servants.

The promise is to us. "But ye are a chosen generation, a royal priesthood" (I Peter 2:9).

7. *Blessing and provision.* The great and rich Abraham had a humble, servant spirit; he was not greedy nor grasping. "And Abram fell on his face: and God talked with him" (Genesis 17:3). When God asked him to give up his only son for a sacrifice, Abraham was willing, but God provided another sacrifice after Abraham showed that all he had belonged to God.

Immediately after this incident, the angel of the Lord told Abraham, "Because thou hast done this thing, and hast not withheld thy son, thine only son: that in blessing I will bless thee, and in multiplying I will multiply thy seed as the stars of the heaven, and as the sand which is upon the sea shore; and thy seed shall possess the gate of his enemies; and in thy seed shall all the nations of the earth be blessed; because thou hast obeyed my voice" (Genesis 22:16-18).

8. *Favor.* "For thou, LORD, wilt bless the righteous; with favour wilt thou compass him as with a shield" (Psalm 5:12). When Esther humbled herself and fought her battle God's way through prayer and fasting, she won the favor of the king. As a result her life and the lives of her people were spared.

9. *Fulfillment.* "If any man will come after me, let him deny himself, and take up his cross, and follow me. For whosoever will save his life shall lose it: and whosoever will lose his life for my sake shall find it" (Matthew 16:24-25). Finding true life is fulfillment in a nutshell.

God has promised to give His servants their desires. "He will fulfil the desire of them that fear him: he also will hear their cry, and will save them" (Psalm 145:19).

10. *Inheritance.* "And whatsoever ye do, do it heartily, as to the Lord, and not unto men; knowing that of the Lord ye shall receive the reward of the inheritance: for ye serve the Lord Christ" (Colossians 3:23-24).

11. *Reward in heaven.* "Behold, I come quickly; and my reward is with me, to give every man according as his work shall be. . . . Blessed are they that do his commandments, that they may have right to the tree of life, and may enter in through the gates into the city" (Revelation 22:12, 14).

In the chapter "Addicted to Serving" we talked about helping the poor (I Timothy 6:17-18). The righteous person who does so has a reward: "Laying up in store for themselves a good foundation against the time to come, that they may lay hold on eternal life" (I Timothy 6:19).

12. *Spiritual prosperity.* In the chapter "Addicted to Serving" we discussed loving in deed rather than merely in word (I John 3:17-18). I John 3:22 gives the reward: "And whatsoever we ask, we receive of him, because we keep his commandments, and do those things that are pleasing in his sight." God blessed Joseph because he had a servant spirit. "And the LORD was with Joseph, and he was a prosperous man. . . . And his master saw that

the LORD was with him, and that the LORD made all that he did to prosper in his hand. And Joseph found grace in his sight, and he served him" (Genesis 39:2-4). Because of his uprightness, Joseph was falsely accused and was cast into prison, but this seemingly disastrous event was the means by which he became the highest ruler in the land next to the king.

We will be rewarded if we keep a servant spirit no matter what position or situation we are placed in, whether it be lowly or high. Servants of Jesus Christ always emerge as winners! They are the cream of the crop. They attain and go forward because Jesus increases in their lives and they decrease. As John said, "He must increase, but I must decrease" (John 3:30). As we decrease, we actually increase spiritually.

Everything people are looking for in life is promised to the servants of Jesus Christ: happiness, fulfillment, prosperity, success, honor, and friends. God's way is definitely the best way, although it is not always the easiest in the short term. The choice is ours: we can follow the road of least resistance and harvest a crop of pain, heartache, dissatisfaction, and dead dreams; or we can choose to let Jesus be the Master and find true fulfillment.

A crown of thorns was placed on His head, shame was associated with His name, and pain and suffering ripped at His heart like a dagger thrust deep and sharp. Why? So we could know joy, glory, success, love, and forgiveness. Do we really have any other choice but to love and serve Him?

The best thing we can do for Him is to let the royal law rule in our lives, which is to love our neighbor as ourselves. As someone once said, "It is good to be saved and know it, but better to be saved and show it."

My fervent desire is that each of us will pour our ointment upon His feet. As Jesus washed the disciples' feet, let us have the same spirit and wash our neighbor's feet. And as the parable of the good Samaritan reveals, our neighbor is anyone who is in need.

CHAPTER 13

Bible Study Outline Servanthood

A. A servant spirit
  1. Matthew 20:25-28
  2. Matthew 23:11-12
B. Three attitudes of a servant
  1. Willingness to serve
    a. Exodus 35:5
    b. I Chronicles 28:9
    c. I Chronicles 29:5
    d. Isaiah 1:19
    e. Proverbs 31:13
    f. I Peter 5:25
    g. Examples
      1. Paul, I Thessalonians 2:6-8
      2. Esther—willing to die
  2. Giving of oneself
    a. II Corinthians 8:1-5

    b. Acts 20:35
    c. Luke 6:38
    d. II Corinthians 9:6-7 (law of harvest)
    e. I Timothy 4:13-15
    f. Mark 14:3-9
    g. Examples
        1. Anna, Luke 2:36-38
        2. Phoebe, Romans 16:1-2
3. Second-mile spirit
    a. Matthew 5:41
    b. Acts 20:24
    c. Romans 12:1
    d. Examples
        1. Rebekah, Genesis 24:17-19
        2. Priscilla and Aquila, Romans 16:3-4

Notes

1. Hy Pickering, *One Thousand Tales Worth Telling*, (London: Pickering & Inglis, n.d.).

2. Herbert V. Prochnow, *The Public Speaker's Treasure Chest* (New York: Harper & Brothers Publishers, New York, 1942).

3. Keith L. Brooks, *Illustrations for Preachers and Speakers* (Grand Rapids: Zondervan Publishing House, 1946).

4. Paul Lee Tan, *Encyclopedia of 7,700 Illustrations*, (Rockville, Md.: Assurance Publishers, 1979).